Dear Parent:

Congratulations! Your child is taking the first steps on an exciting journey. The destination? Independent reading!

STEP INTO READING® will help your child get there. The program offers five steps to reading success. Each step includes fun stories and colorful art. There are also Step into Reading Sticker Books, Step into Reading Math Readers, Step into Reading Phonics Readers, Step into Reading Write-In Readers, and Step into Reading Phonics Boxed Sets—a complete literacy program with something for every child.

Learning to Read, Step by Step!

Ready to Read   Preschool–Kindergarten
• big type and easy words • rhyme and rhythm • picture clues
For children who know the alphabet and are eager to begin reading.

Reading with Help   Preschool–Grade 1
• basic vocabulary • short sentences • simple stories
For children who recognize familiar words and sound out new words with help.

Reading on Your Own   Grades 1–3
• engaging characters • easy-to-follow plots • popular topics
For children who are ready to read on their own.

Reading Paragraphs   Grades 2–3
• challenging vocabulary • short paragraphs • exciting stories
For newly independent readers who read simple sentences with confidence.

Ready for Chapters   Grades 2–4
• chapters • longer paragraphs • full-color art
For children who want to take the plunge into chapter books but still like colorful pictures.

STEP INTO READING® is designed to give every child a successful reading experience. The grade levels are only guides. Children can progress through the steps at their own speed, developing confidence in their reading, no matter what their grade.

Remember, a lifetime love of reading starts with a single step!

Based in part on *The Cat in the Hat Knows a Lot About That!* TV series (Episode 38) © CITH Productions, Inc. (a subsidiary of Portfolio Entertainment, Inc.), and Red Hat Animation, Ltd. (a subsidiary of Collingwood O'Hare Productions, Ltd.), 2010–2011.

THE CAT IN THE HAT KNOWS A LOT ABOUT THAT! logo and word mark TM 2010 Dr. Seuss Enterprises, L.P., Portfolio Entertainment, Inc., and Collingwood O'Hare Productions, Ltd. All rights reserved. The PBS KIDS logo is a registered trademark of PBS. Both are used with permission. All rights reserved.

Broadcast in Canada by Treehouse™. Treehouse™ is a trademark of the Corus® Entertainment Inc. group of companies. All rights reserved.

Visit us on the Web!
StepIntoReading.com
Seussville.com
pbskids.org/catinthehat
treehousetv.com

Educators and librarians, for a variety of teaching tools, visit us at RHTeachersLibrarians.com

Library of Congress Cataloging-in-Publication Data
Rabe, Tish.
Hooray for hair! / by Tish Rabe. — 1st ed.
  p. cm. — (Step into reading, step 3)
ISBN 978-0-375-87048-4 (trade) — ISBN 978-0-375-97048-1 (lib. bdg.) — ISBN 978-0-375-98152-4 (ebook)
1. Hair—Juvenile literature. I. Brannon, Tom. II. Title.
QL942.R33 2012 599.79—dc23 2012005171

Printed in the United States of America
10 9 8 7 6 5 4 3 2 1

STEP INTO READING®

STEP 3

Hooray for Hair!

by Tish Rabe

from a script by Karen Moonah

illustrated by Tom Brannon

Random House 🏠 New York

"Crazy Hair Day in school
is tomorrow," said Nick.
"We need crazy hair
and we both need it quick.
Short on the top?
Or long on each side?
Straight, wavy, or curly?
I just can't decide."

"Did you say crazy hair?"
said the Cat. "Jump in back.
Today I will take you
to visit a yak.
His hair is yak-tastic.
It's shaggy and thick."
"Sounds like a really cool
hairstyle," said Nick.

"Welcome to Hilly Hazair,"
said the yak.
"It's been a long time
and I'm glad you are back."

"You have nice hair,

Mister Yak," Sally said.

"I wish I had hair

just like yours on my head."

"Please," said the yak,

"just call me Yancy.

My hair is shaggy,

but not very fancy."

"If it's yak hair you want,"
said the Cat, "I'll show you
just what my new
Wig-o-lator can do!

"It springs and it sings,
and in just a short while,
it will give both of you
a super hairstyle.

"You'll love your new look!"
The Cat lowered the hood.
"Oh boy!" whispered Nick.
"This is gonna be good."

The Cat pushed a button
and the thing started dinging.
Buzzers were buzzing.
Bells began ringing.

"It tickles!" said Nick.

"This is fun!" Sally said.

"It is putting a wig

on the top of my head."

In less than a minute

both Sally and Nick

had hair like a yak's.

It was shaggy and thick.

"You look great!" said Yancy.

"It's easy to see,

with your thick, shaggy hair,

you two look just like me."

"It's cold here in
Hilly Hazair," Sally said.
"The only thing warm
is the top of my head.
It's fun to have thick hair
like Yancy has got,
but in summer this thick hair
would really be hot."

"Then you'd need hair
of a much different sort.
Like my friend," said the Cat,
"who has hair that is short.

"I will take you
to Blue-Puddle-a-Roo
to meet Celia the Seal.
She can't wait to meet you."

"Hey, Cat!" cried Celia.

"I've been waiting all week."

"Celia," said the Cat,

"has short hair that is sleek."

"Jump in, kids," said Celia.

"The water is fine.

If you're a fur seal,

you need short hair like mine."

"The water's so cold,"
said Sally. "How do you
swim all day long
in Blue-Puddle-a-Roo?"

"I've two layers of hair,"
Celia said. "This is why
though the top one gets wet,
my skin still stays dry.

"I just go jump in
the water, and poof!
I'm warm because
my hair's waterproof."

"On my Wig-o-lator,"
the Cat said, "this wheel
will spin to give you
the hair of a seal!"

"It feels good," said Sally.
"But I just don't know
    if yak hair or seal hair
    is how we should go.

"Long hair is warmer,

but short hair is neat."

"Come on!" said the Cat.

"There's one more friend to meet.

"Here in Poki Moloki

lives a good friend of mine.

His name is Quincy.

He's a fine porcupine.

Quincy has talent.

He's really the best.

He can fluff up his quills

in a porcupine crest."

"Hello, Cat," said Quincy.

"Be careful. Stand back!

My sharp quills protect me

from any attack.

My quills are like hair,

but they're sharp to the touch.

Do you have quills, Nick?"

Nick said, "No, not so much."

"To the Wig-o-lator!" the Cat cried.

"Don't run! Get in line.

And you'll soon have quills

like a fine porcupine.

This is a hairstyle

that everyone likes.

Soon you will each have . . .

". . . a head full of spikes!"

"We look pretty sharp,"

Sally said with a smile.

"But I'm not sure that

porcupine quills are our style."

"It's time to head back,"
said the Cat. "So let's fly!"
"See you later!" said Quincy.
The kids called, "Goodbye!"

"Cat," Sally said,

"before we went to Hazair,

I'd never seen so many

new kinds of hair.

Hair keeps yaks warm

and keeps a seal dry.

Quills protect Quincy,

who's such a nice guy."

"You're right," said the Cat.
"Hair is not just for show.
It can help you stay warm
in the cold winter snow.
It keeps porcupines
from becoming a meal
and helps keep you dry
if you are a fur seal."

"For Crazy Hair Day," said Nick,
"what we'll do
 is have yak hair and seal hair
 and porcupine, too!

"Crazy Hair Day is
going to be great.
Let's both get up early
so we won't be late."

"How was Crazy Hair Day
today?" asked the Cat.
"I wore," said Nick,
"a yak-seal-porcupine hat.
Having yak-seal-porcupine
hair wasn't bad,
but now I'll go back
to the hair . . .

"... that I had!"